Four Polish Folk Songs

for Flute and Piano
(2009, 2014)

Arranged by
Jon Jeffrey Grier

Piano Accompaniment

for Marion

Copyright © 2021 LudwigMasters Publications (ASCAP).
International Copyright Secured. All Rights Reserved.

Program Notes

I. Hej Sokoly (Hey Falcons)

Hej Sokoly is about beautiful, green Ukraine and a Ukrainian girl, to whom her Polish boyfriend says goodbye for the last time. Its origins are unknown. It was sung during the Polish-Soviet War by soldiers and also by the Home Army guerillas during World War II. After the war it was adopted by the Polish Boys Scouts, and today it has become one of the better known hits from the repertoire of the folk music group Biesiada. Text by Polish Ukrainian poet Tymko Padura (1841-1971), along with Juliusz Slowackie represents the so called Ukrainian school in Polish Literature.

Hej Sokoly

Żal, żal za dziewczyną, za zieloną Ukrainą,
Żal, żal serce płacze, już cię nigdy nie zobaczę.
Hej, hej, hej sokoły, Omijajcie góry, lasy, doły,
Dzwoń, dzwoń, dzwoń dzwoneczku, Mój stepowy skowroneczku.
Hej, hej, hej sokoły, omijajcie góry, lasy, doły,
Dzwoń, dzwoń, dzwoń dzwoneczku,
     mój stepowy dzwoń, dzwoń, dzwoń...
Ona jedna tam została, jaskółeczka moja mała,
     na zielonej Ukrainie, przy kochanej tej dziewczynie.
Hej, hej, hej sokoły... Wina, wina, wina dajcie,

Hey Falcons

Pity, pity, pity for the girl, and for
the Green Ukraine.
Pity, pity, the heart it weeps, for I shall never see you
Hey, hey, hey, but the falcons skip over the mountains,
the forests, and holes in the ground...
So ring, ring, ring the bell, my prarie lark.
Well she's the only one that stayed there,
My little swallow, on the Green Ukraine
Next to that lovely, lovely girl.
Give me wine, wine, wine, and if I die,
Bury me there, on the Green Ukraine
Next to that lovely, lovely girl.

II. Na Wojtusia Z Popielnika (A Little Spark)

This is a traditional lullaby melody with words by the poet Janina Porazinska (1888-1971)

Na Wojtusia Z Popielnika

Na Wojtusia z popielnika
Iskiereczka mruga
- Chodź opowiem ci bajeczkę,
Bajka będzie długa.

Była sobie raz królewna,
Pokochała grajka,
Król wyprawił im wesele...
I skończona bajka.

Była sobie Baba Jaga,
Miała chatkę z masła,
A w tej chatce same dziwy...
Cyt! iskierka zgasła.

Patrzy Wojtuś, patrzy, duma,
Zaszły łzą oczęta.
Czemuś mnie tak okłamała?
Wojtuś zapamięta.

Już ci nigdy nie uwierzę Iskiereczko mała.
Najpierw błyśniesz, potem gaśniesz,
Ot i bajka cała.

A Little Spark

A little spark is winking
at Wojtus from the cinders
come, let me tell you a story,
the story will be long.

There was once a princess
enamored of a singer,
the king made them a wedding,
and the story ends here.

Once there was a witch,
she had a little hut made of litter;
And in this hut,
there were only strange things!

Pssst! The spark went down.
Wojtus looks and muses,
His eyes filled up with tears:
- Why did you fool me so? I'll remember that!

I won't ever believe you! You little spark!
You shine for a moment, then you go down!
And that's it - the whole story.

III. Na wierzbowym listku (Ada's kujawiak #1)

The *kujawiak* is a dance from the region of Kujawy in central Poland on the Mazovian plains; it is one of the five Polish national dances. It is characterized by its misplaced accents, usually on the second or sometimes the third beat of the bar. In Ada Dziewanowska's *Polish Folk Dances and Songs* (1997), the *kujawiak* is described as danced with a calm dignity and simplicity, in a smooth flowing manner "reminiscent of the tall grain stalks in the fields swaying gently in the wind." It has a slightly slower tempo than the *mazurka*, which comes from the neighboring region of Mazowsze, and to which it is likely related. This melody is sometimes referred to as *Ada's Kujawiak No. 1*

Na wierzbowym listku
Na wierzbowym listku słowik list pisze,
a gdy już napisał, przerwał wiatr ciszę,
przerwał listek, przerwał, zanićosł go wiośnie,
potem przysiadł na sośnie.

I skinęła ręką i wnet wyszło słońce,
słowik strzepnął piórka i połące
dana, dana poszła piosnka
od samego rana.

Księżyc już się jasną czapką chmur skłonił,
kiedy wiosna listek wzięła w swe dłonie,
przeczytała słowa, w których był smutek,
żal słowika i nuty.

The Nightingale and the Willow Leaf
The Nightingale wrote a letter on a willow leaf,
when he finished it the wind interrupted the silence,
the Nightingale cut off the leaf and carried it to spring
and then sat on a pine.

Spring waved her hand and the sun came out,
the Nightingale fluttered his feathers
and a song "dana, dana" burst forth in the meadow
on that morning.

The moon already bowed with his light cap of clouds
when Spring took the leaf in her hands
and read the words which contained
the sadness and sorrow of the Nightingale,
and musical notes.

IV. Krakowiak

The *Krakowiak* is a fast, syncopated dance in duple time from the region of Kraków. The steps of this dance mimic the movements of horses, which were well loved in the Kraków region of Poland for their civilian and military use. It became a popular ballroom dance in Vienna ("*Krakauer*") and Paris ("*Cracovienne*")—where, with the *polonaise* and the *mazurka*, it signaled a Romantic sensibility of sympathy towards a picturesque, distant, and oppressed nation. Frédéric Chopin produced a bravura concert *krakowiak* in his Grand Rondeau de Concert *Rondo à la Krakowiak in F major* for piano and orchestra (Op. 14, 1828). (Wikipedia)

About the Arranger

Jon Jeffrey Grier holds a B.A. from Kalamazoo College, where he studied composition with Lawrence Rackley, an M.M. in Composition from Western Michigan University, studying with Ramon Zupko, and an M.M. in Theory and a D.M.A. in Composition from the University of South Carolina, where he studied with Jerry Curry, Dick Goodwin and Sam Douglas. Jon taught Advanced Placement Music Theory and Music History at the Greenville Fine Arts Center, a magnet school of the arts in Greenville, SC from 1988 to 2019, where he was named Teacher of the Year three times. Awards include grants from ASCAP, the Surdna Foundation, the South Carolina Music Teachers Association, the Metropolitan Arts Council, and the Atlanta Chamber Players. Jon has also been a writer/keyboardist in various jazz & fusion ensembles since 1984. He lives in Greenville with wife Marion and Carolina Dingo Roxanne.

FOUR POLISH FOLK SONGS
I. Hej Sokoly

Traditional
arranged by Jon Jeffrey Grier

© Copyright 2021 LudwigMasters Publications, LLC • ALL RIGHTS RESERVED
Digital and photographic copying of this publication is illegal

with tap pedal

both hands

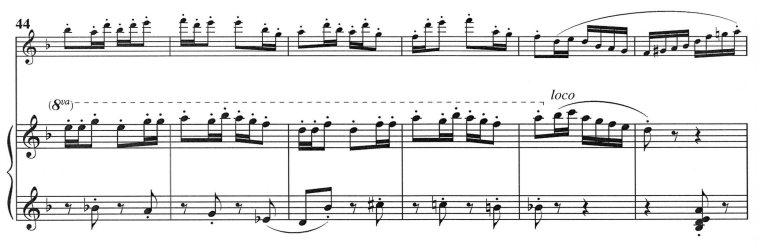

loco

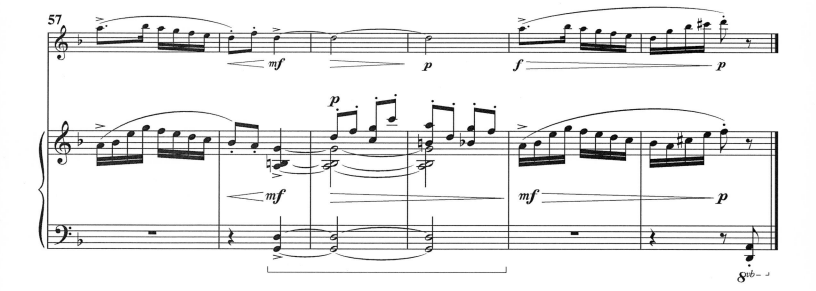

II. Lullaby: Na Wojtusia Z Popielnika

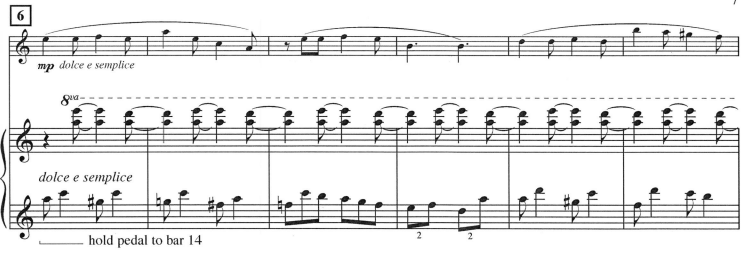

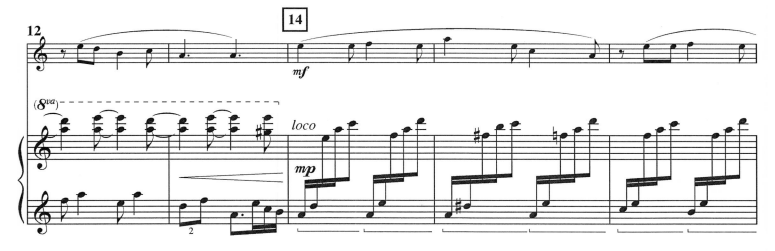

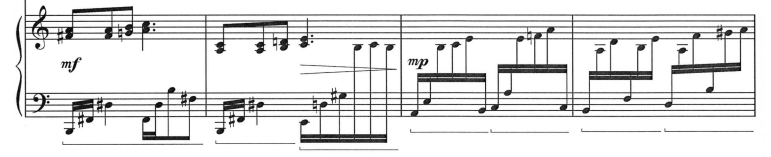

III. Kujawiak

Flute

FOUR POLISH FOLK SONGS
I. Hej Sokoly

Traditional
arranged by Jon Jeffrey Grier

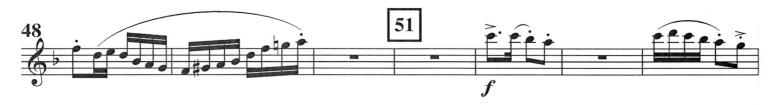

© Copyright 2021 LudwigMasters Publications, LLC • ALL RIGHTS RESERVED
Digital and photographic copying of this publication is illegal

50410008

II. Lullaby: Na Wojtusia Z Popielnika

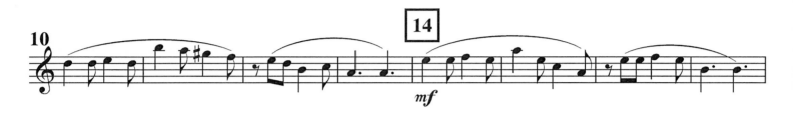

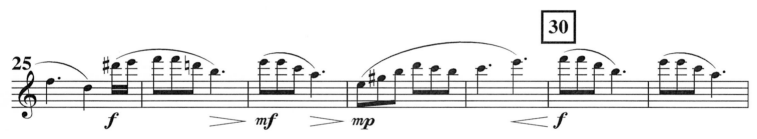

Flute

III. Kujawiak

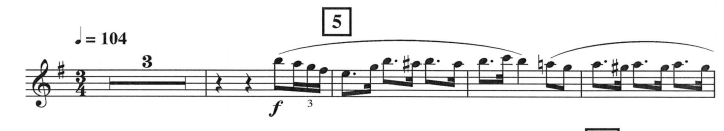

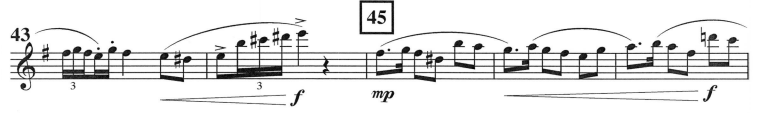

50410008

IV. Krakowiak

Flute

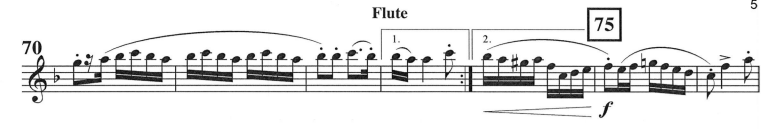

50410008

Program Notes

I. Hej Sokoly (Hey Falcons)

Hej Sokoly is about beautiful, green Ukraine and a Ukrainian girl, to whom her Polish boyfriend says goodbye for the last time. Its origins are unknown. It was sung during the Polish-Soviet War by soldiers and also by the Home Army guerillas during World War II. After the war it was adopted by the Polish Boys Scouts, and today it has become one of the better known hits from the repertoire of the folk music group Biesiada. Text by Polish Ukrainian poet Tymko Padura (1841-1971), along with Juliusz Slowackie represents the so called Ukrainian school in Polish Literature.

Hej Sokoly
Żal, żal za dziewczyną, za zieloną Ukrainą,
Żal, żal serce płacze, już cię nigdy nie zobaczę.
Hej, hej, hej sokoły, Omijajcie góry, lasy, doły,
Dzwoń, dzwoń, dzwoń dzwoneczku, Mój stepowy skowroneczku.
Hej, hej, hej sokoły, omijajcie góry, lasy, doły,
Dzwoń, dzwoń, dzwoń dzwoneczku,
      mój stepowy dzwoń, dzwoń, dzwoń...
Ona jedna tam została, jaskółeczka moja mała,
      na zielonej Ukrainie, przy kochanej tej dziewczynie.
Hej, hej, hej sokoły... Wina, wina, wina dajcie,

Hey Falcons
Pity, pity, pity for the girl, and for
the Green Ukraine.
Pity, pity, the heart it weeps, for I shall never see you
Hey, hey, hey, but the falcons skip over the mountains,
the forests, and holes in the ground...
So ring, ring, ring the bell, my prarie lark.
Well she's the only one that stayed there,
My little swallow, on the Green Ukraine
Next to that lovely, lovely girl.
Give me wine, wine, wine, and if I die,
Bury me there, on the Green Ukraine
Next to that lovely, lovely girl.

II. Na Wojtusia Z Popielnika (A Little Spark)

This is a traditional lullaby melody with words by the poet Janina Porazinska (1888-1971)

Na Wojtusia Z Popielnika
Na Wojtusia z popielnika
Iskiereczka mruga
- Chodź opowiem ci bajeczkę,
Bajka będzie długa.

Była sobie raz królewna,
Pokochała grajka,
Król wyprawił im wesele...
I skończona bajka.

Była sobie Baba Jaga,
Miała chatkę z masła,
A w tej chatce same dziwy...
Cyt! iskierka zgasła.

Patrzy Wojtuś, patrzy, duma,
Zaszły łzą oczęta.
Czemuś mnie tak okłamała?
Wojtuś zapamięta.

Już ci nigdy nie uwierzę Iskiereczko mała.
Najpierw błyśniesz, potem gaśniesz,
Ot i bajka cała.

A Little Spark
A little spark is winking
at Wojtus from the cinders
come, let me tell you a story,
the story will be long.

There was once a princess
enamored of a singer,
the king made them a wedding,
and the story ends here.

Once there was a witch,
she had a little hut made of litter;
And in this hut,
there were only strange things!

Pssst! The spark went down.
Wojtus looks and muses,
His eyes filled up with tears:
- Why did you fool me so? I'll remember that!

I won't ever believe you! You little spark!
You shine for a moment, then you go down!
And that's it - the whole story.

III. Na wierzbowym listku (Ada's kujawiak #1)

The *kujawiak* is a dance from the region of Kujawy in central Poland on the Mazovian plains; it is one of the five Polish national dances. It is characterized by its misplaced accents, usually on the second or sometimes the third beat of the bar. In Ada Dziewanowska's *Polish Folk Dances and Songs* (1997), the *kujawiak* is described as danced with a calm dignity and simplicity, in a smooth flowing manner "reminiscent of the tall grain stalks in the fields swaying gently in the wind." It has a slightly slower tempo than the *mazurka*, which comes from the neighboring region of Mazowsze, and to which it is likely related. This melody is sometimes referred to as *Ada's Kujawiak No. 1*

Na wierzbowym listku
Na wierzbowym listku słowik list pisze,
a gdy już napisał, przerwał wiatr ciszę,
przerwał listek, przerwał, zanićosł go wiośnie,
potem przysiadł na sośnie.

I skinęła ręką i wnet wyszło słońce,
słowik strzepnął piórka i połące
dana, dana poszła piosnka
od samego rana.

Księżyc już się jasną czapką chmur skłonił,
kiedy wiosna listek wzięła w swe dłonie,
przeczytała słowa, w których był smutek,
żal słowika i nuty.

The Nightingale and the Willow Leaf
The Nightingale wrote a letter on a willow leaf,
when he finished it the wind interrupted the silence,
the Nightingale cut off the leaf and carried it to spring
and then sat on a pine.

Spring waved her hand and the sun came out,
the Nightingale fluttered his feathers
and a song "dana, dana" burst forth in the meadow
on that morning.

The moon already bowed with his light cap of clouds
when Spring took the leaf in her hands
and read the words which contained
the sadness and sorrow of the Nightingale,
and musical notes.

IV. Krakowiak

The *Krakowiak* is a fast, syncopated dance in duple time from the region of Kraków. The steps of this dance mimic the movements of horses, which were well loved in the Kraków region of Poland for their civilian and military use. It became a popular ballroom dance in Vienna ("*Krakauer*") and Paris ("*Cracovienne*")—where, with the *polonaise* and the *mazurka*, it signaled a Romantic sensibility of sympathy towards a picturesque, distant, and oppressed nation. Frédéric Chopin produced a bravura concert *krakowiak* in his Grand Rondeau de Concert *Rondo à la Krakowiak in F major* for piano and orchestra (Op. 14, 1828). (Wikipedia)

About the Arranger

Jon Jeffrey Grier holds a B.A. from Kalamazoo College, where he studied composition with Lawrence Rackley, an M.M. in Composition from Western Michigan University, studying with Ramon Zupko, and an M.M. in Theory and a D.M.A. in Composition from the University of South Carolina, where he studied with Jerry Curry, Dick Goodwin and Sam Douglas. Jon taught Advanced Placement Music Theory and Music History at the Greenville Fine Arts Center, a magnet school of the arts in Greenville, SC from 1988 to 2019, where he was named Teacher of the Year three times. Awards include grants from ASCAP, the Surdna Foundation, the South Carolina Music Teachers Association, the Metropolitan Arts Council, and the Atlanta Chamber Players.   Jon has also been a writer/keyboardist in various jazz & fusion ensembles since 1984. He lives in Greenville with wife Marion and Carolina Dingo Roxanne.

Selected Flute Publications

METHODS

BAKER, JULIUS
Cox, Alan

10300130   Daily Exercises for the Flute (Grade 4)
A terrific and valuable collection of exercises for advanced flutists, the studies in this book are intended to build a high degree of technical solidity by means of intensive work on scale, scale patterns, seventh-chord progressions, thirds, sixths, chromatic sequences, fast staccato, high tones, and various duet selections. By diligent and careful work on these daily exercises, students will build a flawless tehcnical foundation on the flute, and more advanced players will keep themselves in shape.

COLLECTIONS

BALENT, ANDREW
50341003   Classical Solos (Grade 2.5)

HARRIS, FLOYD O.
50341006   Competition Solos, Book 3 Flute (Grade 3.5)
A practical collection of competition solos for young instrumentalists, many of which are on state festival lists. The piano book includes alternate accompaniments for instruments of different pitch and therefore can be used for any instrument in the book three series. Titles included: Brass Bangles; Caprice; Dancing Silhouettes; Evening in the Country; Ocean Beach (Valse); Polka from Bartered Bride; Viennese Sonata No. 4 (Rondo)

HARRIS, FLOYD/ SIENNICKI, EDMUND
50341005   Competition Solos, Book 2 Flute/Oboe (Grade 2.5)
Book 2 is a practical collection of competition solos, many of which are on state festival lists. Piano book includes alternate accompaniments for instruments of different pitch and therefore can be used for any instrument in the book two series. Titles included: The Young Prince; Viennese Sonatina No. 1 (Allegro); Flower of the Orient; The King's Jester; Two Short Pieces; Spirit of Victory; Barcarolle and Scherzetto; Sparkles; Waltz from Album for the Young.

KERKORIAN, GREGORY M.
50341008   Easy Orginal Flutes Duets and Trios
Beautifully written and arranged with the young player in mind, these duets and trios make wonderful concert and festival repertoire for early performance.

SOLO, UNACCOMPANIED

ADLER, SAMUEL
10410523   Canto XIII for Flute (Grade 4)
Adler, Samuel. Published by Ludwig Music, Cleveland,. Copyright 1994. A rare piece for solo piccolo, this work may be performed straight, or the player may make dramatic entrances and theatrical gestures.

FERROUD, PIERRE OCTAVE
M284891   Three Pieces

SIENNICKI, EDMUND J.
10340101   Recorder Fun (Grade 1)

SOLO WITH PIANO

BACH, J.S.
Marteau, Henri

10410234   Andante Cantabile (Grade 3)
Andante Cantabile [Sinfonia Concertante in E-flat for Two Violins and Orchestra: Andante]

BRICCIALDI, GIULIO
Davis, Albert O.

10410186   Carnival of Venice for Flute and Piano (Grade 4)
This famous melody in theme-and-variations form features a marvelous cadenza. Its technical challenges are dazzlingly impressive!

BUSSER, HENRI
M114291   Petite Suite

M298091   Prelude Et Scherzo

CASELLA, ALFREDO
M266891   Barcarola E Scherzo

M371291   Sicilienne and Burlesque

CHAMINADE, CECILE
M114791   Air De Ballet: Seren

DEBUSSY, CLAUDE
M168591   Clair De Lune

GANNE, LOUIS
M127091   Andante Et Scherzo

GAUBERT, PHILIPPE
M186691   Deux Esquisses

M122791   Nocturne Et Allegro

M196191   Sicilienne: Madrigal

M218391   Sonata In A

M297991   Suite (Grade 4)
This suite, by renowned French flutist Philippe Gaubert, is in four movements, with each movement dedicated to a master flutist of the time. It is a fine contest or recital selection for the advancing musician. Movements: I. Invocation (danse de pretresses), II. Berceuse Orientale, III. Barcarolle, IV. Shzerzo-Valse

GERMAN, EDWARD
M330491   Suite

GLIERE, REINHOLD
M330691   Two Pieces, Op.35

GRIFFES, CHARLES TOMLINSON
M282291   Poeme

HAHN, REYNALDO
M342491   Two Pieces

HARTY, HAMILTON
M292591   In Ireland

HUE, GEORGES
M152191   Fantaisie (Grade 4)
Composed for the Paris Conservatory 1913 and later orchestrated in 1923, Hue's Fantasie is a beautiful work for the advancing flutist. The piece begins with a spacious and atmospheric Assez lent section, which is complimented by intricate melodic lines on the flute. This introduction leads into a beautiful Modere section and concludes with a rousing Tres vif encore.

REINECKE, CARL
W100891   Concerto Op. 283

ROSENHAUS, STEVEN
P001791   Rescuing Psyche
Rescuing Psyche for flute and piano was commissioned by the Music Teachers National Association and the NYSTMA and was premiered by flutist Kelly J. Covert and pianist Nathan Hess. Rescuing Psyche takes its inspiration from Greek mythology. Eros, a god, and Psyche, a mortal, are in love, but Aphrodite is jealous. Aphrodite successfully traps the mortal in a coma, but Eros wakes his love by playing a flute. The flute part has some key clicks and flutters but no other extended techniques or special effects are required.

WIDOR, CHARLES-MARIE
M183591   Suite, Op. 34

TRIO

KOECHLIN, CHARLES
M333291   Three Divertissements

Exclusively Distributed by
Alfred Music
LEARN · TEACH · PLAY

Questions/ comments? info@keisersouthernmusic.com

IV. Krakowiak

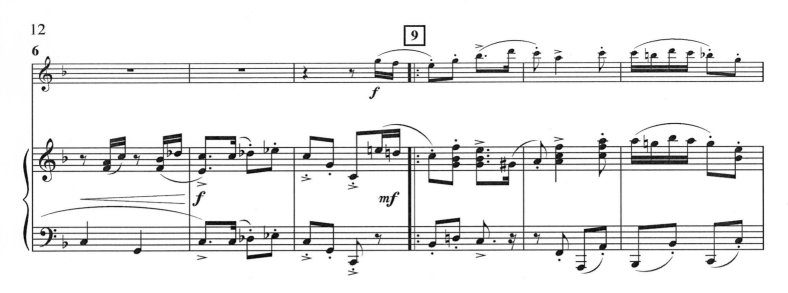

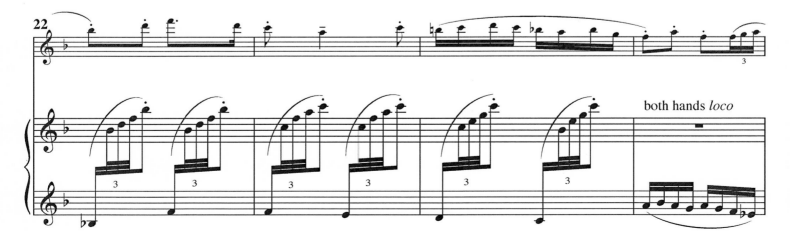

14

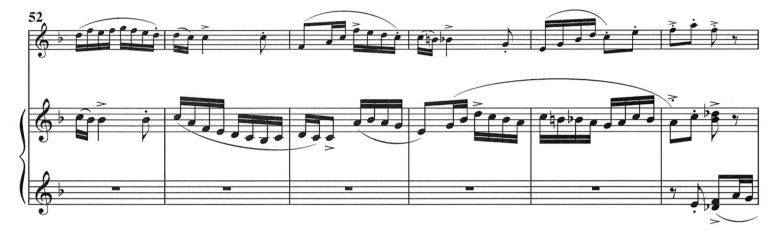

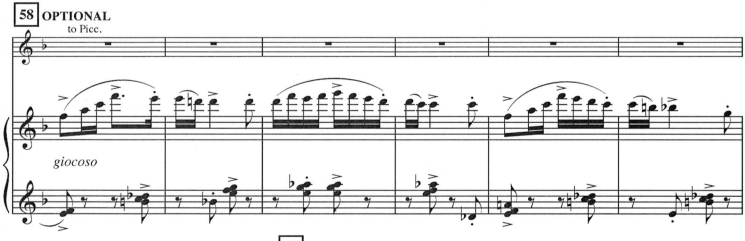

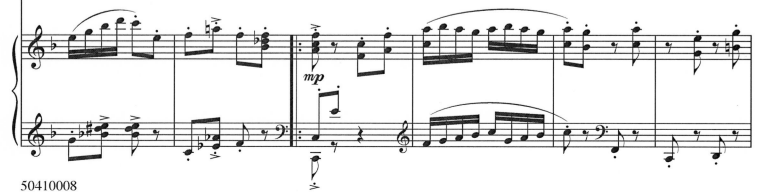

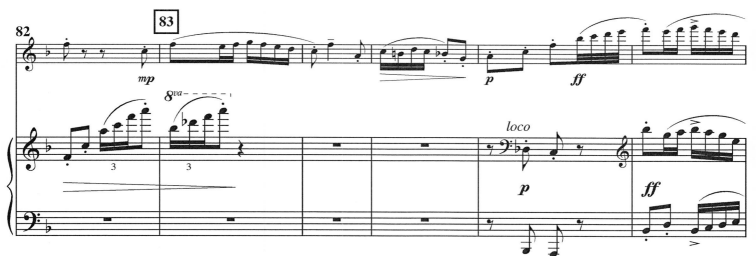

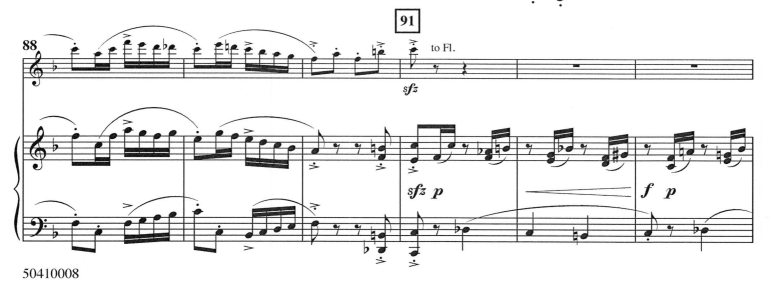

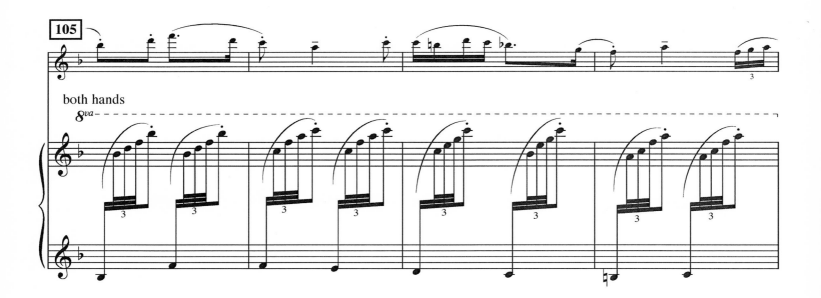

Selected Flute Publications

METHODS

BAKER, JULIUS
Cox, Alan

10300130   **Daily Exercises for the Flute (Grade 4)**

A terrific and valuable collection of exercises for advanced flutists, the studies in this book are intended to build a high degree of technical solidity by means of intensive work on scale, scale patterns, seventh-chord progressions, thirds, sixths, chromatic sequences, fast staccato, high tones, and various duet selections. By diligent and careful work on these daily exercises, students will build a flawless tehcnical foundation on the flute, and more advanced players will keep themselves in shape.

COLLECTIONS

BALENT, ANDREW

50341003   **Classical Solos (Grade 2.5)**

HARRIS, FLOYD O.

50341006   **Competition Solos, Book 3 Flute (Grade 3.5)**

A practical collection of competition solos for young instrumentalists, many of which are on state festival lists. The piano book includes alternate accompaniments for instruments of different pitch and therefore can be used for any instrument in the book three series. Titles included: Brass Bangles; Caprice; Dancing Silhouettes; Evening in the Country; Ocean Beach (Valse); Polka from Bartered Bride; Viennese Sonata No. 4 (Rondo)

HARRIS, FLOYD/ SIENNICKI, EDMUND

50341005   **Competition Solos, Book 2 Flute/Oboe (Grade 2.5)**

Book 2 is a practical collection of competition solos, many of which are on state festival lists. Piano book includes alternate accompaniments for instruments of different pitch and therefore can be used for any instrument in the book two series. Titles included: The Young Prince; Viennese Sonatina No. 1 (Allegro); Flower of the Orient; The King's Jester; Two Short Pieces; Spirit of Victory; Barcarolle and Scherzetto; Sparkles; Waltz from Album for the Young.

KERKORIAN, GREGORY M.

50341008   **Easy Orginal Flutes Duets and Trios**

Beautifully written and arranged with the young player in mind, these duets and trios make wonderful concert and festival repertoire for early performance.

SOLO, UNACCOMPANIED

ADLER, SAMUEL

10410523   **Canto XIII for Flute (Grade 4)**

Adler, Samuel. Published by Ludwig Music, Cleveland,. Copyright 1994. A rare piece for solo piccolo, this work may be performed straight, or the player may make dramatic entrances and theatrical gestures.

FERROUD, PIERRE OCTAVE

M284891   **Three Pieces**

SIENNICKI, EDMUND J.

10340101   **Recorder Fun (Grade 1)**

SOLO WITH PIANO

BACH, J.S.
Marteau, Henri

10410234   **Andante Cantabile (Grade 3)**

Andante Cantabile [Sinfonia Concertante in E-flat for Two Violins and Orchestra: Andante]

BRICCIALDI, GIULIO
Davis, Albert O.

10410186   **Carnival of Venice for Flute and Piano (Grade 4)**

This famous melody in theme-and-variations form features a marvelous cadenza. Its technical challenges are dazzlingly impressive!

BUSSER, HENRI

M114291   **Petite Suite**

M298091   **Prelude Et Scherzo**

CASELLA, ALFREDO

M266891   **Barcarola E Scherzo**

M371291   **Sicilienne and Burlesque**

CHAMINADE, CECILE

M114791   **Air De Ballet: Seren**

DEBUSSY, CLAUDE

M168591   **Clair De Lune**

GANNE, LOUIS

M127091   **Andante Et Scherzo**

GAUBERT, PHILIPPE

M186691   **Deux Esquisses**

M122791   **Nocturne Et Allegro**

M196191   **Sicilienne: Madrigal**

M218391   **Sonata In A**

M297991   **Suite (Grade 4)**

This suite, by renowned French flutist Philippe Gaubert, is in four movements, with each movement dedicated to a master flutist of the time. It is a fine contest or recital selection for the advancing musician. Movements: I. Invocation (danse de pretresses), II. Berceuse Orientale, III. Barcarolle, IV. Shzerzo-Valse

GERMAN, EDWARD

M330491   **Suite**

GLIERE, REINHOLD

M330691   **Two Pieces, Op.35**

GRIFFES, CHARLES TOMLINSON

M282291   **Poeme**

HAHN, REYNALDO

M342491   **Two Pieces**

HARTY, HAMILTON

M292591   **In Ireland**

HUE, GEORGES

M152191   **Fantaisie (Grade 4)**

Composed for the Paris Conservatory 1913 and later orchestrated in 1923, Hue's Fantasie is a beautiful work for the advancing flutist. The piece begins with a spacious and atmospheric Assez lent section, which is complimented by intricate melodic lines on the flute. This introduction leads into a beautiful Modere section and concludes with a rousing Tres vif encore.

REINECKE, CARL

W100891   **Concerto Op. 283**

ROSENHAUS, STEVEN

P001791   **Rescuing Psyche**

Rescuing Psyche for flute and piano was commissioned by the Music Teachers National Association and the NYSTMA and was premiered by flutist Kelly J. Covert and pianist Nathan Hess. Rescuing Psyche takes its inspiration from Greek mythology. Eros, a god, and Psyche, a mortal, are in love, but Aphrodite is jealous. Aphrodite successfully traps the mortal in a coma, but Eros wakes his love by playing a flute. The flute part has some key clicks and flutters but no other extended techniques or special effects are required.

WIDOR, CHARLES-MARIE

M183591   **Suite, Op. 34**

TRIO

KOECHLIN, CHARLES

M333291   **Three Divertissements**

Exclusively Distributed by
Alfred Music
LEARN • TEACH • PLAY

Questions/ comments? info@keisersouthernmusic.com